MEN
AND SHEDS

GORDON THORBURN

MEN
AND SHEDS

CONTENTS

SHEDS AND SHEDDISTS

Let us begin in the Dark Ages and in a shady place, because the modern English word "shed" comes from the Anglo-Saxon for shade, *scead*, pronounced "shay-ud", which is how they still say it in certain northern districts of England.

Scead, of course, means partial darkness or comparative obscurity. These are fundamental concepts in understanding what made a Sheddist originally. He was a kind of wise man, a hermit, an oracle. He was partially dark and comparatively obscure but ordinary folk knew he was different, in a very special way.

Over the years, the old concept of shed – hermit's retreat – developed extra shades of meaning. The hermit assembled things around him, some with magical significance. He collected strange objects, the importance of which others could not understand, and worked on them with his hands. His shed became his intellectual pantry, his workshop, his spiritual home.

7

Some of the Sheddists in this book have chosen to interpret this ancient tradition to the letter and stay in their sheds all day, every day, making a living at it. There are potters who pot, inventors who invent, a chap who sings 'Crystal Chandeliers' all the time, a fellow who carves ducks and swans, and a poltergeist hunter.

For others, the shed itself is the thing and the way it's kitted out. There's the British Railways guard's van restored to glory, and the fisherman's grotto, and the state-of-the-art recording studio.

Some men are obsessed by the unusual items they put in their sheds. Some have made their sheds their social hub, inviting the like-minded inside to share that certain whatever-it-is. Some have not the slightest idea and don't care a jot or tittle. For many, though, it's the escape thing. They admit it. A hobby might be the raison d'être on the surface but, as they say on "The X Files", the truth is in there.

HOW DID IT EVOLVE?

Scientists may postulate that Sheddism, like ginger hair and sticky-out ears, is genetic. This book contains evidence for such a proposal, for example, the man whose uncle made the first wireless set in their street. Contrarily, there is also evidence for the Big Bang theory as with the man who, unaware of the life-shaping importance of his action, picked up a brick on the beach.

Most Sheddists and Sheddism experts do, however, agree on a quite different premise, which is to do with sex. In these days of political correctness, such an issue is difficult and dangerous to face but it is clear that the ladies, bless them, are simply not in the shed. Is this because they lack the Shedding instinct, or is it something more sinister?

Are blokes Sheddists only by consent? Perhaps the ladies allow us to construct our hideaways so we can escape from the house and get away from her indoors.

9

MIRROR, MIRROR, ON THE SHED WALL

We have to ask each Sheddist to examine the following scenes. Is there anything here, anything at all, which you recognise and which therefore might help us with our inquiries into the nature of Sheddism?

The women do it by hints. Sometimes the hint is no more than the flicker of a seductive eyelash, a slight pursing of the lips, or that special little tickly thing she does with her index finger on the end of your nose.

Sometimes it's a few words, spoken subtly and without any kind of imperative. These words might be along the lines of "How are you getting on with your glider/milk bottles/steam engine/working model of Space Station Mir made entirely out of grass clippings?"

Or, she might say "How do you expect me to get on with my womanly, feminine tasks with a great fat useless idle ugly wart like you under my feet the whole time?"

If we chaps are being dismissed to our sheds, why is that? Why have they not moved in beside us? They play our Rugby League, spot our train numbers, understand the offside and LBW laws – what's going on?

SHEDDISM -V- MODERNISM

Things accumulate in sheds, originally wanted then forgotten and much later resurrected as momentous mementoes. Old magazines like *Picture Post* for instance. A favourite of mine had an advert for a car showing a standard American family admiringly boarding a huge and ugly late 1950s car, under the headline "We're not the richest folks in town. We just look it."

Sheddists are not outraged by this impossibly naïve drivel. Sheddists smile at the idea of everyone in town writing you begging letters and asking you to be mayor, just because you have seated yourself in a colourful carriage of bent tin resembling a shark-shaped jukebox.

Signs hung on shed walls say things like *Guinness is good for you*, *Craven 'A' cigarettes will not harm your throat* and *Bovril prevents that sinking feeling*, invalid scientifically but so what? The public once was given credit for common sense. They got the message without believing the advertisement. Nowadays, while the rest of the world has gone barking mad, Sheddists retain that traditional sense of what is right and good.

SHEDDISM AND QUIET ENJOYMENT

As a very small boy, your correspondent lived in a village in north Yorkshire where father was the village policeman. The house had no mains water but it did have a shed, up the field.

Regular use was made of this shed which was fitted with a small, pale wooden roller hanging on a piece of rusty wire and a polished wooden seat with a large hole in it. A man came to empty the shed every once in a while.

In that golden age, although sound and music were not yet the norm of the world, a shed was still a welcome refuge. Today, those who seek peace and quiet might be regarded as slightly odd by those norms who revel in constantly available music plugged into their ears, broadcast in their cars, at work and, crime of crimes, in the pub, but that's what sheds are all about. Here's to tranquillity.

Gordon Thorburn

"CORKSCREW STARBOARD – GO!"

...as the WW2 gunners used to order their bomber pilots when they were attacked by a fighter. One day, Lyndon will make his shed-top gun turret rotate so he can take evasive action while shooting imaginary Junkers 88s. Meanwhile, he's busy with his seven-piece visual orchestra, the Busk-O-Matic. His players (see picture: Lyndon is the one in the middle) blow smoke rings, bubbles and showers of sparks.

Lyndon's day job is managing and flying aerial surveys, like the one precisely mapping new routes for London's tube. When he returns to his shed it's his mind which is flying, producing a string of world firsts: the propeller-powered wickerwork car, the amphibious bathchair, the amphibious tricycle and the world's first conversion of a 1922 Citroën to wickerwork (yes, he likes wickerwork).

If anyone has a pair of Browning .303 machine guns for the turret, contact: www.lyndonsmachines.co.uk.

"It's crackers but is it art?"

SHOP AT SHEDCO

Members of the Golders Green Allotment and Horticultural Society can fulfil all their earthy needs in the Gardeners' Bazaar, whose honorary proprietor is John, aged 84. Managing the enterprise, catering for 196 allotments, is second nature to someone who used to manage a large bakery.

Golders Green's north London oasis is a long way from Gold Beach, Normandy, on D-Day, where John was with the 8th Army Royal Engineers, but his army training is still useful. Now he has the mowers, rotavators and strimmers to maintain, bought with shop profits and hired out to members.

John's three-shed terrace, at the posh end of the shed spectrum, has stucco walls, a tiled roof and mod cons. The shop and storage are full of what every gardener wants – seeds, compost, canes, cloches, green string – and the office has what every horticultural provisioning executive deserves: a microwave and a kettle.

"We had 5 plots in 1913 – before my time of course."

HANDY ON THE ETHIOPIAN BANJO

Jim was an engineer making street lights. Illness forced him to retire so he turned himself into a highly skilled and remarkably expressive woodcarver.

Finding the wood at a decent price is difficult. He likes lime best – it must be very well seasoned – but he also works in oak. See the two old boys sitting on a bench? The one with the stick is Jim's late father-in-law, and the full-size stick is the duck's head by Jim's left hand, with a hazel shaft, a lime head, a mahogany beak, and a home-made nut and bolt to fix it together.

There is no design to start with. He looks at the wood and waits for an idea to come out of it, like the great hall with rooms off, the corral or the charioteer. Then he just sits in his chair in his shed, carving away or, for a change, renovating his friend's Ethiopian banjo. Young Albert's stick with the horse's head handle might have been the finest that Woolworth's could sell, but Jim sells nothing. To carve is the thing.

"I started when I heard 'Albert and the Lion'."

THE GARDENER'S ARMS

There'll be an analytical chemist somewhere who can prove that the atomic composition of a supermarket leek, sprout or runner bean is identical to that of your own allotment leek, sprout or runner bean. Scientists? They should stick to inventing the voice-activated doorknob.

True anti-scientists Dink, Robbo and Prem (reading from the left), are seen here meeting in the lounge bar of The Gardener's Arms for an organic discussion on the relative merits of Amsterdam Forcing and Chantenay Red Cored as general-purpose carrots in a dampish climate. As usual, the conversation has broadened into even more vital issues such as global warming, the price of hand-rolling tobacco and whether the Old Foxwhelp cider-apple tree needs supplementing, perhaps with a Strawberry Norman.

Provided the fuel for the stove lasts out and the homemade refreshments likewise, conviviality could persist into the late afternoon, making gardening completely unnecessary for another day.

"Stringless, with smooth, fleshy pods."

ORDOVICIAN IS THE WORD

While the first backbones were evolving into something approaching a fish, Martin's raw material was being formed. Called brick shale, this grey clay is Ordovician, 450 million years old, and is so rough it will take your skin off if you throw it on a wheel.

Ordinary clay, made more recently by glacial grinding, cannot give Martin the same feelings, nor can it offer the same challenges to his clients when, after admiring the lovely red it has become in firing, they try to lift the work they've commissioned. Large clay sculptures are normally hollow. Martin's brick shale sculptures are solid, limited in size only by the capacity of the kiln.

For smaller work, he still won't allow convention into his converted coalhouse. He likes Raku, the Japanese method of taking the item out of the kiln red hot and plunging it into sawdust. He gets more brightly coloured glazes that way.

"A Winged Victory for your garden?"

THE WORST LPs IN THE WORLD

Plastics company manager John is definitely in the escaping category of sheddists, keen to get away from the TV and the phone. He built the shed himself entirely out of old pallets with insulated double walls, extension and porch – but to his wife's orders. John uses the shed himself – but has to listen to his wife's choice of music.

Because of her 1950s fixation, this means John is an expert on Alma Cogan, Anne Shelton, Ronnie Hilton and so on, and he cordially hates them all. 'Songs that Won the War' is probably his least favourite, making him dive for the fitted refrigerator where the beer is kept. Wine and spirits are in the tasteful kitchen cupboard to his left. Friends come for meals in the winter, heated by John's stove which he brought back from France on a rugby bus. They reminisce about wooden tennis racquets, Bakelite telephones, 'Two-Way Family Favourites' and 'Music While You Work'. They should probably get out more.

"Homely cozy junk, really."

SHED IN THE PARK

Richard was a management accountant and university teacher but it's woodwork which satisfies his soul. After teaching himself the range of techniques, he's now happily making window frames, kitchen units, furniture, anything.

His house is called the Shippon – an old English word for cowshed – but his woodworking shed is his masterwork. Were it not in a National Park it would by now be a bijou residence. It had been used as a garage and Richard had to go through the planning hoops to be allowed to restore it back to a shed.

His best find was the wall which had been knocked down to make the garage doors. That was under the concrete floor. Richard dressed the stone and, with some lintels from a reclamation yard, his own windows and doors and stone flags in front, it's beginning to look rather upmarket, really. Still, nothing's too good for the sheddist classes.

"The house is the cowshed. The shed is no house."

ONE PUNCH BEYOND

Stephen's expanding paranormal activities have forced a move out of the house and into the garden shed. He's an expert on UFOs (mostly experimental aircraft, he believes) and parapsychology – the study of extrasensory perception. His growing reputation brings him work from the most unlikely quarters.

A council tenant complained about water in the house appearing from nowhere. Water is a regular feature of poltergeist infestation, which is usually connected with stress in those being infested. Stephen managed to collect some of this water. Laboratory tests showed it to have 30 times the normal reading for conductivity units. It was, literally, electrified.

On another poltergeist job, in front of two witnesses, Stephen received a mighty blow in his back which sent him flying, "like a punch combined with an electric shock. It's OK investigating but it's a bit much when the investigator becomes the victim."

"There's a rational explanation, usually."

IF IT CAN BE FIXED, IT WILL BE

Sheet steel is expensive. People throw washing machines on tips. Therefore, mend your Renault 4 rustbucket with rectangles of washing machine. This is a philosophy which Robin applies in his garage and which he takes with him into his shed.

His wife seems to be the main source of supply for his shed work. While Robin collects every kind of screw, nut, bit and piece in the world by dismantling every thrown-out food mixer or lawnmower that comes his way, his beloved brings home things she finds in skips, charity shops and car-boot sales. She knows that he will have the ability and the wherewithal to fix whatever, and she likes to keep him busy.

From rebuilding an exercise bike to mending jewellery to fixing a leather binding to making a buffing machine for antique brass, Robin is the man who can. One of his uncles built the first wireless set in his street. It's in the blood, that sort of thing.

"I'd quite like to read a book, really."

"I SLEPT WITH HARRY SECOMBE...

...in the same tent, when we were in the Army. We were part of the excitingly named Central Pool of Artists, along with Ken Platt, Norman Vaughan and others. I was a magician. Harry was a singer, gradually turning himself into a comedian."

Ralph at 78 and a member of the Magic Circle for 55 years, doesn't perform his magic professionally any more. He prefers to pass on his secrets to aspiring youngsters, fellows of the ancient Manchester Order of the Magi.

From magic to origami to plastic moulds for decorations may seem a curious route but it's all arts and crafts and that is Ralph's forte. He supplies play schemes, youth clubs and community projects with his moulds, produced on a vacuum-forming press in his shed, from originals he's made himself, or found. The moulds are virtually indestructible – a bit like Ralph.

"My act used to be the drunk with the lamp-post."

A PROFUSELY DRILLED SKIRT

The pile of bits on the floor of Hicky's shed included the front axle, the 4.3 litre 4-cylinder engine, the gear box and a few other useful items. The rear axle and the chassis were elsewhere, somewhere, and there was no bodywork at all, or wheels, but these were minor inconveniences compared to the exciting possibility of rebuilding the oldest competition Sunbeam in the world (see picture).

Hicky says this is the works hill-climb car, one of only three 1911 Sunbeam 16/20s left. He made the aluminium body, following photographs and a contemporary description which gave it a profusely drilled skirt. He made the wicker seats, too. Hicky's friends say they can't tell where his shed stops and his house begins, which may be something to do with the various states of repair of his 1903 Peugeot, 1909 Cadillac, 1913 Star, 1916 5.7 V8 Cadillac, 1917 Dodge, 1928 hill-climb special Riley/Rover and other evidence, if it were needed, of his life-long fascination. And, at intervals, he is still heard to murmur 'Poop-poop!'

"I'm a sporting person, not a polishing person."

WHAT'S THE DIFFERENCE BETWEEN A DUCK?

One leg is both the same, of course, which rather sums up Guy's route through life. He designed a lady's head on a stick for a level-crossing sign, to make people notice it more. Another dark, driftwood head was stolen by children who left it propped up against a front door and almost frightened a poor old lady pensioner to death.

Such matters seem inevitable to Guy, who discovered his gift for wood-art while minding the ducks in Regent's Park. He started with a small axe, making decoy-type ducks, and people wanted to buy them, so it was but a short step to mute swans (stylised, see picture), West End galleries, magazine articles and TV.

He's withdrawn a little now, to the gentler lights of small local galleries, but he still has the same approach. He likes estuary driftwood but he doesn't look for shapes inside it. He wants a big block that he can draw and cut out with a bandsaw. How do you make a duck? Well, you get a piece of wood and you...

"...chop everything off that don't look like a duck."

150 LIGHTS AND 2000 CRYSTALS, OR SMALLER

When Joseph arrived in the UK from Iraq he didn't know what an antique was and he'd never seen a chandelier. A job in an antique shop led to chandeliers in his bedroom and, soon, to a shed. He had to build it. There's a limit to how many chandeliers you can get in a bedroom.

There's a limit in the shed, too, but Joseph doesn't want to step beyond it for the moment. He's happy going to antique fairs in Belgium and France, buying the chandeliers of old, restoring them and selling them to a never-ending line of customers who prefer to deal with him rather than a big company.

In the line recently was a Saudi sheikh who wanted his 1860 French Empire £150,000 chandelier done up and hung. It measured twelve metres by eight, which is three times bigger than Joseph's shed. Otherwise, Joseph's customers are everyday town and country folk who just happen to fancy some *fin de siècle* twinkling grandeur in the sitting room, at a modest price.

"My style, not just any old chandelier."

THE SECRET LIFE OF A TAXMAN

Out of his shed, he is exactly like an ordinary chap. He goes to the office (Inland Revenue), works, comes home, leaves stuff lying about the house and gets moaned at by his wife for making the place untidy. Then, he goes to his shed and is transformed. Terry, in the cramped confines of his workshop, becomes Super Orderly Recycling Man.

Every tool has its hand-carved peg so, when finished with, it can hang at perfect right angles to its neighbour. Every project, unless *in extremis*, is made with left-over this and that. A left-over door became some new flooring in the house, a left-over bedside cabinet became a wall-mounted display case, bits of left-over timber became a model aeroplane and a folding table with model race track attached. The chimney breast in the dining room, left over after the central heating was installed, became a built-in Welsh dresser. Left over from his youth is a Sun calendar for 1984. It's on his shed wall, permanently open at Linda Lusardi.

"We're awash with CDs, but I've wood left over."

SELL, OR OPEN A MUSEUM?

John started small with steam before moving into combustion engines. His first was a Lister D petrol/paraffin which, in the old days, drove the vacuum pump which milked the cows in just about every milking parlour in the country. Lister made 600,000 of these static engines, used to power everything imaginable, and taking his to a rally was enough to set John in search of bigger, rarer and increasingly challenging machines.

His biggest was a 16HP Crossley Horizontal, 35cwt, which drove the cast-iron rollers in a mortar pan, crushing ashes and lime into powder. His rarest was a Boulton and Paul from 1924. John also built all four of his sheds but, after falling off the roof of one, breaking his back and his neck, he will not be building any more. His injury also means he can't cart the really big engines around to exhibit, so some of the collection, if it's to be seen, must be sold. The one in the picture he classes as medium – a 5HP Petter, originally used to drive a concrete mixer. But what's that thing in the corner?

"It's a searchlight off a fire engine."

BRICK TRIGGERS CLICK

Scientists believe that dozens of behavioural traits lie latent within everyone, waiting for that unexpected sight or sound to flick the switch. For many of us, the stimulus to brick collecting never operates. For Angus it did, in 1989. He can tell you when, and where – walking along a beach – he first picked up a brick, but he cannot tell you why.

Once started, he couldn't stop. He didn't care about the small gangs of children running after him, hoping he was looking for money. Having scoured his own locale pretty well, Angus now sets off in his car to beaches, demolition sites, old collieries and fly tips where he may find a duplicate, to be kept outside the shed for swapping with other collectors (yes, there are several), or a specimen he's never seen or heard of before. His interest is not in every Tom, Dick and Harry of a brick. Only those with makers' names and marks are deemed suitable for recording by sketch and note in his catalogues. He likes to be able to classify them by place of origin and to list them by county.

"But I'm quite happy just to have them."

45

TALK, WALK AND CHARGE AT THE SAME TIME

Trevor was no great scholar but he could produce the most astounding essays with his Meccano set. That's the way his mind works, translating dreams into practical reality by way of an engineer's hands and ten thousand washing machine components. The shed provides the space and wherewithal to put the invention, the idea he couldn't mention in case they laughed, which became that bizarre contraption spread all over the bench, into a box which can then be called a product.

It was in his shed that the famous clockwork radio was invented. More recently it's been the electric shoe, which puts a small recharge into your mobile phone battery every time you put one foot in front of another. Also rechargeable is the device which fits in your ear and teaches you basic English for an hour, 'you' being – for starters anyway – 140 million Chinese. A few words of English can transform a life in such a country. Trevor's ideas are like that. For more inspiration, attend the inventors' forum on www.thetbf.org.uk

"I give myself enough room to be original."

THE ART OF THE UNIVERSE

Fifteen years ago, you would have needed a million dollar telescope, a massive building and a mainframe computer to do what Alan does. Now, for rather less than the cost of small car, he has the technology and the purpose-built observatory, artfully designed to look exactly like a garden shed so it fits in with the flowers that surround it.

His reflecting telescope is moved about the sky by software Alan has written himself. We can see only two galaxies with the naked eye: our own Milky Way and Andromeda, a mere two million light years away. Alan's looking three or four hundred million light years away, at the thousands of galaxies which exist up to that distance. There are billions more but, for the moment, you still need the million dollar job to see them. His built-in camera system takes digital images of his galaxies and these pictures are his real passion. Not for him the endless search for a new comet. He prefers the beauty of the known but, until recently, invisible universe. See his pictures on www.ajefferis.freeserve.co.uk

"10" Schmidt-Cassegrain, SBIGST7e CCD and AO."

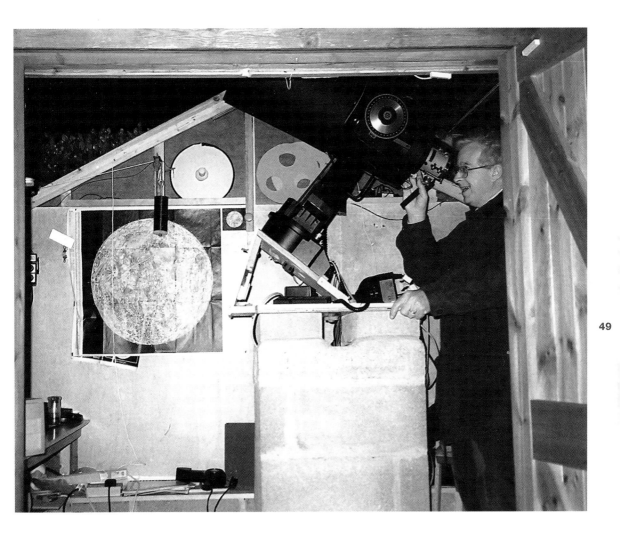

THE SIMPLE LIFE, WITH HEALTH AND SAFETY

"Beware of the scribes, which love... the chief seats in the synagogues and the uppermost rooms at feasts." St Mark's Gospel 12:38, could hardly have foreseen the plight of a Suffragen Bishop of the Church of England who, rather than a palace, is given an ordinary detached house with no room for a chapel.

"For which of you, intending to build a tower, sitteth not down first, and counteth the cost, whether he have enough to finish it?" Good advice there, then, from St. Luke's Gospel 14:28. A nice cheap shed will do for the Bishop's contemplation and it will echo the simplicity of the early Christians who had no cathedrals and stained glass.

Nevertheless, if it is to shelter the public – and there's reasonable room for half a dozen, with the record set at 16 – there are various health and safety regulations about heating and so on. No problem. After rendering unto Caesar that which is Caesar's, the good Bishop can find stillness and prayer in his garden refuge.

50

"You don't get much space as a Bishop."

A MEADOW OF WILD FLOWERS

...just as it was 100 years ago, is a priceless jewel in cool Britannia. From building oil rigs through to community work in Papua New Guinea, via many connections between, Tom has landed on a smallholding which hasn't seen any changes in a century.

The cottage is 300 years old and, during the restoration, whether it is a kitchen cupboard or a five-bar gate, if it is possible to make it, Tom makes it in his shed. The policy is strict: local materials, sustainable development, traditional methods and designs, no negative impact on the environment. Tom believes in the opposite of globalisation; to rely on your local environment makes you respect it and care for it.

He also believes in the opposite of modern farming. They use artificial fertilisers and devote themselves to monoculture. For Tom, biodiversity is what Nature intended and farming should be in tune, not in conflict.

"My neighbour said, you going to plough it, then?"

HISSING SID EATS BATTY BAT

Well, not bats exactly, but mice the snakes certainly eat, and rats, rabbits, guinea pigs, chicks – all bought frozen, plus rainbow trout as a treat for the crocodiles. Stillborn lambs are a hit with the Burmese pythons.

The common iguana normally hangs out in trees overlooking water, into which it will unhesitatingly plunge if disturbed. This one prefers Andy, who also has about 40 pythons in his shed, various other lizards, and a dozen or two venomous cobras of both the striking and the spitting kinds. He has a boa constrictor which was thrown over the wall of an animal rescue centre on a December day, which he has nursed back to full health.

Andy's ambition is to breed his biggest animals, a pair of Asian reticulated pythons. He will use temperature and humidity to imitate their home seasonal cycle, which is quite an art. Then he'll introduce them in their early Spring and hope that a young reticulated python's fancy lightly turns to thoughts of love.

"Do not disturb the iguana."

EVERYWHERE, WE'RE BATTERED BY SOUND

The small, frail, balsa and tissue paper model aeroplane, with its rubber band motor, is launched with a whirr and a slight rattle into the breeze by its nervous maker. To his satisfaction and surprise, the aircraft climbs and, as the twists in the rubber run out, glides slowly back to earth with the sun glinting on its shiny, painted wings.

This mental picture, taken by Gordon when he was thirteen, stayed with him through the years until, retired, he could set about recreating it. His aircraft are bigger now. Some are radio-controlled gliders for slope-soaring. Others have electric motors, powered by batteries for almost silent running.

He doesn't make them too big – six feet wingspan or so – because he likes to take them on holiday in the car. His wife can paint her watercolours while Gordon goes soaring in silence. The quietness matters to him. It's peaceful in his shed, making something that he can watch as it flies without a sound, the sun glinting on its shiny, painted wings...

"There's no noise in a standing wave of air."

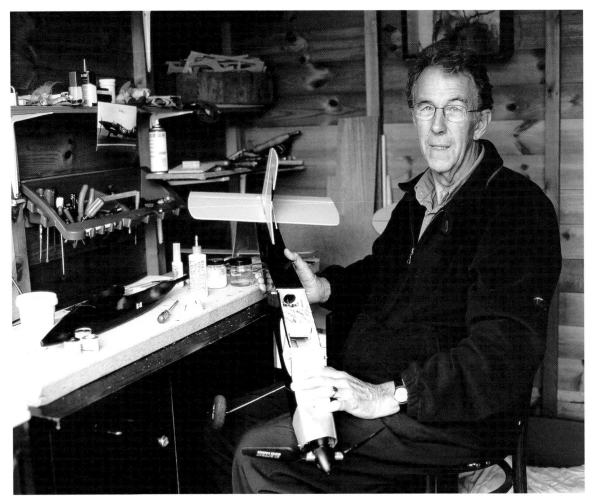

YO HO HO AND A BOTTLE OF PINOT NOIR

The base for the shed had already been built by the time they moved to their new house on the Friday morning. The wood arrived on the Friday afternoon and John had the shed shell built by the Sunday. It took him a few more August evenings to do all the fiddly bits but the shed was ready for inaugural ceremonies within the week.

It's a drinking shed, and a theme shed. A beachcombing friend brought a fisherman's net back and the tone was set. Like all theme pubs it is tacky but, in John's case, connoisseurs must appreciate the post-tacky irony with which it is furnished. Friends and family who feature in the list of those privileged to enjoy its facilities bring sea-going treasures back from around the world – a set of shark's teeth, ships in bottles, fancy shells, wall plaques, sea-urchin ash trays, plaster of Paris dioramas of the boy standing on the burning deck, all good stuff like that. And, it doesn't matter if anyone spills a drink because it goes through the floor rather than staining the carpet.

"Have you seen my papier mâché dolphin?"

LET THE SUN SHINE IN

Strictly and formally speaking, the term 'crane' – used because of a resemblance to the bird of that name – refers only to the arm or jib of the mechanism used for lifting heavy weights and displacing them horizontally. Patrick makes that bit out of old bean tins.

By 'crane' we now mean the whole thing, including the cabin, made of papier mâché, and the tracks, made of six dozen cheap 2-inch hinges soldered together. It's a kind of rebirth for Patrick. He used to drive cranes, including the one he's modelling, a 22RB Rushton Bucyrus, the perfect machine renowned throughout the Empire for sand and gravel digging.

Twenty years ago he built his shed, carefully designing it to catch the sun with south-facing, upward tilting windows. He paints it with sump oil every time he gives his car a service then, safe from rot and woodworm, he gets on with his other winter project – recycling bicycles from old wrecks that have been chucked out.

"I make one good 'un out of three."

MAN EMBARRASSES WIFE ON A1

Almost all milkmen say a thankful goodbye to their bottles at the end of their rounds. One who doesn't is Ken. He likes milk bottles so much that he pays good money for them, such as £100 for one of three known examples of the bottle with the actress Zoe Newton pictured on it. Another collector paid £300 for the only one in brown glass.

Ken's collection of about 4,000 bottles, housed in his shed, is small to middling. Some have 10,000, and exchange is good business in Milk Bottle News, a publication yet to feature on BBC2's 'Have I Got News For You' but which boasts a circulation literally over 90. Quality is what matters and Ken's best resource is the Great North Road. He scours the hedge backs for bottles thrown away by lorry drivers of the past. He might find a Blyth Co-op bottle with a 3-colour advert for orange juice. Or he might just embarrass his wife, who sits in the car in the lay-by with her head in the glove box, while Ken does his thing in the ditch.

"Most of my friends are bottle collectors."

YOUNG FARMER WAITS PATIENTLY

The Bedford OW short wheelbase tipper, 1944, never got to the war it was built for. Instead it worked for the council, then on a farm in the marshes, and a lad saw its nose sticking out of a barn and offered £25 for it. It was 12 years before truck and money were finally exchanged and Mick could get on with restoration in his shed, itself a war veteran originally meant to house barrage balloons.

Along with his 500cc BSA single pot, his Velocette noddy bike and his Singer Gazelle, the truck is used for fun runs and kept in working order rather than as an untouchable museum piece.

Mick's other passion is growing beef like beef used to be, from proper British breeds. He sells it through his local butcher, where people queue up for the meat the supermarkets won't let them have, which gives him a great deal of satisfaction, along with his vehicles, his organic farming methods, living in the house he was born in, and the old ways.

"It's a lovely place for owls."

POTTING SHED, MAN AND BOY

Michael was a boy potter – five-year apprenticeship at a big pottery firm, £5 a week. He worked his way through to be head thrower in the factory but, after 20 years, with more and more machinery coming in, he began to feel underused.

It became clear that there was no place for a skilled man in a modern pottery factory. A few throwers were kept for display to visitors, but that was all. A shed was the answer, a big shed which used to be part of a bakery, and here he embarked on his mission to defeat the march of the machine. He knew all there was to know about throwing clay but that was all he knew. He had to learn the rest and so, at weekends, he taught himself firing, glazes, putting handles on, all those things.

Michael now has stands at Bakewell market and York and Stratford-on-Avon. Water features, bird feeders, all sorts. All handmade, in his shed.

"The terracotta frog goes down well."

THE SHED'S A FINE AND PRIVATE PLACE...

...usually, but here's one which opens to the public. David, smitten by films since he was old enough to watch one, had a personal cinema in the spare room. When they moved house he had to start again, with a new shed, soundproofing, ten seats from the local Odeon, a projection booth and an eight-foot screen.

Every two weeks, a group of OAPs came in for a film show. This was a full programme, with cartoon, tea and biscuits – there will now be a short intermission – everything. Alas, the old 8mm projector was creaking after 20 years and so David went technological. His video projection system produces sound and vision exactly like the old real thing, except you can't hear the clicks.

He gets his 'Coming Shortly' posters from the big cinema when they've finished with them. The OAPs still turn up every fortnight, and his friends from the quiz team. Well, it's not everybody who has a picture house in his garden.

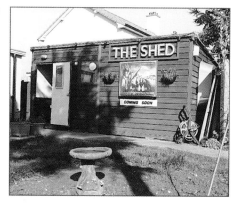

"TV? Films weren't meant for TV."

"I TOLD YOU SO" SAID THE TOAD

The crowd holds its breath as Noah's Ark, the ship built to save the living planet, slides down the slipway. She reaches the water... She's tipping over... She sinks. "I told you it wouldn't float" says a toad spectator, his voice powered by a reprogrammed birthday card insert.

Welcome to Ron's world, the toymaker extraordinaire, who has spent virtually all of his working life in his shed, dreaming up comic fantasies and constructing the intricate means to make them perform. At the moment, lions and marigolds preoccupy his thoughts as he builds an automaton for the local hospital, for the room where children wait for their minor operations.

They'll be able to turn a handle and watch a moth take off from the flowers. The lion follows it with his eyes and goes cross-eyed as it lands on his nose. He sneezes. The moth flits away. The lion tries to catch it, gives up, and the moth settles once more on the marigolds.

"Turn the handle, watch the story."

HE'S GOT THE WHOLE WORLD IN HIS SHED

Does your herd of 150 Fresians need milking? Perhaps you've had a slate or two sucked off your roof by the gale. Possibly a dead elm tree is posing a threat to your upstairs windows, or maybe the windows need new panes of glass, or coats of paint, or the sash weights don't work.

While you are on holiday, your goats/geese/ducks/pigs have to be fed. Winter is drawing near. You must find someone with a tractor and trailer who will cut up the said elm tree for logs. It's spring. The garden needs digging, the new patio needs laying, the washing machine has broken down, the kitchen tap is dripping, the stairwell must be papered, that bit of wall needs rendering and the lawnmower won't start. The septic tank is blocked, the water main is leaking, the chickens need a new hut building, the back field needs fencing, the hay must be baled, the car needs a service, the tumble drier is overheating. For almost any of life's little difficulties, all you need is Eric, chairman, managing director and workforce of Flemco International. One man and his shed.

"Me and my shed, O."

I'VE GOT A LUVVERLY BUNCH OF COCONUTS

Dave comes from a long line of travelling showmen and was brought up on the fairgrounds. He and his brother had a set of gallopers (roundabout to you), and a set of dodgems, and overboats. The family home was a caravan for many years until, like so much from the old days, the modern world didn't seem to want them any more.

Dave, now over 80, builds replicas of the showmen's living waggons, much bigger than the gypsy horse-drawn types because they were made to be pulled on good roads by steam traction engine and, later, by lorry. Dave pulls his on a trailer behind his camper van, when he and his wife go to the steam rallies to help raise money for charity.

For those of you watching in black and white, Dave is sitting beside a quarter-size model of his aunt's caravan painted in green, yellow and gold. He's made every little bit of it himself, in his shed.

"We packed it in and went on the tarmacadam."

SIMPLY MADE AND CRUDELY FINISHED

Richard's day job is writing software for palm pilots but he has a genetic compulsion towards his shed. Inheriting a collecting and constructional streak from both grandfathers gives him an irresistible urge to make Pat's crocodile back-pack, John's square and rubbery weekend pants, Wendy's briefcase with stainless steel hawser handles and a coffee table which moves about on three tricycle wheels.

This not so much art trouvé as parts trouvés. He sees a pile of old cylinders, links it with his T-shirt storage problem and conceives the idea of a mild steel wardrobe (see picture). It may look like an enemy of Dr Who but it is a perfectly functional home for Richard's smalls and it has his preferred rough look. Donna's doorknocker, the scary alien's head table and the landing gear chairs are all viewable now at www.jarkman.co.uk. He offers to take on commissions but this would surely mean a potential client having an equal urge, without the constructive skills, towards an office chair with motorcycle shock absorbers or a stereo amplifier with gaspipe and cog. Wouldn't it?

"Anybody want a lunar barbecue?"

WATCHING WALES IN BLACK AND WHITE

Everything in Geraint's personal third of his shed terrace has to be found, not bought. His hermit's cell, therefore, is furnished with a sofa nobody wanted and his TV for watching the rugby is black and white. He admits this can be an advantage if you don't want to see the shirt colour of the team scoring all the tries.

Geraint is a great planner. With three small children he could see his space in the house shrinking and so sketched out his idea of a proper shed, 20 feet long, and took it to the local sawmills. They obliged and so Geraint, a big chap, has the room not to feel squashed. The stone wall is to protect the shed from footballs (what happened to rugby?) when the kids are not in their own third of the shed.

The smallest, third portion, in the middle, is ostensibly for mundanities such as garden tools but was actually designed as a buffer zone. It is fitted with a double forcefield, preventing invasion, which can only be breached by shouting "JPR, where are you now?"

"I wanted something significant in the garden."

SHED MAN CURES VIKING'S DISEASE

In 1964, a young bricklayer called Brian was working alone, cutting some stone with an angle grinder. The machine kicked and sliced almost through his right wrist. Luckily, he was near a hospital and managed to stagger into A&E a moment before he collapsed through loss of blood.

They sewed his hand back on but he spent 30 years, driving HGVs and buses, with two fingers clawed up. Then he developed Dupytren's Contracture (Viking's Disease) in his left hand, all of which clawed up. The large, cumbersome, painful splints used to try to straighten the hand were intolerable and so Brian sat down in his shed and invented a new type. It's small and flexible. It straightens the fingers at rest but allows the hand to grip. Surgeons and occupational therapists all over the world are queuing up. Hospitals in Scandinavia, Germany and the USA are already using it and the rest of the world will follow. There have been great difficulties, with official bureaucracy and sourcing components but Brian has overcome them all. It's amazing what a shed man can do.

"It's a world beater, this is."

GEEZERBIRD IN RED LIGHT DISTRICT

Green musicians in a recording studio like Abbey Road are apt to be struck by Red Light Fever – the inability to perform under the financial and clock-ticking pressure of the dreaded red 'Recording' light.

Phil, well aware of this phenomenon from his own experience, has converted his garden shed into a fully-functioning, fully-equipped, state-of-the-art studio. He offers himself and his gear to the young and talented at modest, non-pressurising fees.

Phil can also offer advice about the long and winding road to musical fame. His own band is Geezerbird, fronted by his singer/songwriter partner who – he says – does geezerish things on rockfaces while he stays home and sees to the ironing. A cross between Blondie and The Eurythmics, they've made their single and their video, they've done the pubs and clubs, Phil's made a dance remix of their song – called, inspirationally, Geezerbird – but stardom knocks not. Yet.

"I love being behind the twiddly buttons."

GED'S ORDINARY SHED

Among this plethora of elaborate sheds and eccentric owners, how refreshing to find someone completely normal. Gerard, known as Ged, has spent his working life surrounded by dozens of other people's children, trying to teach them the difference between King Lear and a dangling participle. Naturally he likes to escape to a small wood and glass box, surrounded by dozens of varieties of deep-rooting and aggressive prairie grasses, where he can sit and consider his next move.

Should he lash out a few quid on six Capsicum **F1** Redskin pepper seeds, to grow in pots? He ponders, in his scholarly way, the text on the packet, which pictures a glossy marvel of a plant tumbling with shining red peppers. 'Sunny border or well placed tub' it says. Ged realises that they have accidentally omitted the words 'in Acapulco or Cyprus'. So, what will happen? Sow six seeds, four show, one nibbled by snail, plant three in pots, blackbird pulls one up, remaining two die from sheer misery one cold afternoon or wither because he forgot to water them. No, Ged thinks, he'll leave that for now.

"Say it with vegetables."

LOVE AT FIRST SIGHT

There they were, Chris and his wife, having a normal day out, when a vision of loveliness went past. He fell immediately, truly, madly, deeply. She was also enthusiastic. So it was that they made a promise to each other. One day, when they settled down and had a garden big enough, they would have an old British Railways guard's van as a shed.

The idea is one thing. Obtaining a decrepit 1956 Darlington guard's van is quite another, not to mention building a platform for it to stand on, finding and fixing railway lines and sleepers, paving the lawn with planks so the 50-ton crane can go there to lift the van into the garden through a gap where a row of trees used to be, and restoring it. The right sort of wood came out of a Victorian coach. The paint is the proper stuff in BR Freight Brown. The pot-bellied stove and chimney are precise replicas. It's nearly finished. They both think it's great. The children are going to have sleep-outs in it.

"Barbecue. In guard's van if wet."

IS THAT WHAT THEY'RE FOR?

You have a large, two-level apartment for several modern, young, busy, artistic metropolitans to share. Downstairs are the living quarters where folk that pass in the night and morning can briefly nod their acquaintance. Facilities here are much as might be expected: jacuzzi, potato peeler, toasting fork, coal scuttle, flight simulator, dolly tub, bread-making machine, recordings of steam trains going up the Lickey Incline. Some of that may not be quite right but you know the sort of thing.

The difficulty arises above. It's open plan. Modern metropolitans cavil at dorm living, so what do they do? They tried partitions. Room dividers don't transpose to the average warehouse floor. Luke, visiting a certain well known DIY store in search of jacuzzi powder, had a Damascene experience. There, before him, in cedar and creosote, were things of beauty which also offered him the practical solution to the privacy problem. "You got a big garden, then?" asked the lady at the store. "No" said Luke. "You got lots of small gardens, then?" she said. "No" said Luke.

"They're for upstairs."

SHED HEAVEN

Our 17th century farmhouse in Westmorland had eight acres, half a mile of trout stream and, as they say around there, sheds amain.

The one to make you jealous would be the 19th century sandstone haybarn. It was about 160 feet long and 40 feet wide, with a stone ramp up to the hayloft floor, below which were the original cattle byres.

In this our Great Shed we kept chickens, bred Golden Retrievers and stored the new village hall which was a second-hand Finnish wood prefab, to be erected as soon as... well, soon.

Incorporated in the Great Shed was the bull pen, where we kept pigs, fattened geese and succoured orphan lambs. Beside that was my tractor shed with garden tractor and trailer, early ride-on mower, antique rotavator, deadly brush cutter and all associated tools and rubbish. In the milking parlour (c.1950) we kept our furniture, moving it into the house as we worked through nine years of restoration.

Next to the house was a row of single-storey stone buildings looking like ancient cottages for Scottish peasants. The end one fell down. Next was the old smithy, where our friend Eric (qv) kept all his stuff, then The Cabin, where the farmer's wife used to cook for the men. Here I had DIY tools, timber, bags of cement, hand-wrought nails, circular saw and all sek mak o' tackle, and my fishing gear. Next came the log shed, the animal feed shed, and the old dairy where my wife kept her stock for her fruit and nut business and where lived Smartie and Muswold, the two cats charged with the protection of said stock.

We also had a proper hen hut in the front field, and Goose Hall. Now it's only a 1960s single garage and a three-roomed Victorian cellar...

"A shedless man is a kiss without a moustache."

PHOTOGRAPHER JOHN BAXTER AND SHED

"Photography opens the door to meeting a lot of people and seeing a lot of things you wouldn't normally see" says John, a man who's seen more of Britain than most.

His CV includes work for clients as varied as *Crafts Magazine* and *Oasis Holiday Villages*, paintings and antiques catalogue photography, and collaborative projects with Gordon Thorburn on village cricket and the Appleby Rai. His favourite, however, is his profile of a champion leek grower from County Durham, who thanked him with a gift-box of enormous prize vegetables.

Between shoots, there are the pleasures of family life – wife of eight years, Johanne, and son Jack, who's two – and the stresses of supporting Blackburn Rovers. And, when he needs to get away from it all, he goes fell walking – well, unless it's raining, in which case there is always his shed.

There he can relax between the growing stack of radiators and the pile of paint rollers, and contemplate the coat of whitewash he's intending to give the walls in the very near future...

But, then, that might ruin the rugged ambience of the interior, and photographers are obsessed by these minutiae.

"Thorough, but not particularly organised."

PHOTOGRAPHER LAURA FORRESTER AND SHED

Just as Surrey, her county of birth and residence, combines cityscape and countryside, so Laura has covered a varied plot of photographic territory over the course of her short career.

Right from childhood days in her father Paul Forrester's studio, she always wanted to be a photographer. Her favourite project to date, "Bums", which she completed as part of her degree in Photography at Blackpool, is a large composite of prints, featuring the bottoms of twelve fellow students. Apparently, it tends to provoke a lot of interest.

So from backsides to back gardens: this is her first commercial project, which has taught her you can never judge a shed by its exterior... nor the blokes who own them.

Inspired by her visit into the inner sanctum of blokedom, she is already developing her own garden shed into something more than a junk repository. It's a modest but cosy affair, complete with net curtains at which most die-hard shed-men might wag a disapproving finger. But she insists she's not girlie. And she's not afraid of getting muddy.

"It's just another room of the house."

Reprinted in 2003
First published in 2002 by
New Holland Publishers (UK) Ltd
London • Cape Town • Sydney • Auckland
www.newhollandpublishers.com

Garfield House
86-88 Edgware Road
London W2 2EA
United Kingdom

80 McKenzie Street
Cape Town 8001
South Africa

Level 1, Unit 4
Suite 411, 14 Aquatic Drive
Frenchs Forest, NSW 2086
Australia

Unit 1A, 218 Lake Road
Northcote, Auckland
New Zealand

10 9

Editor: Gareth Jones
Editorial Direction: Rosemary Wilkinson
Designer: Paul Wright
Photographers: John Baxter, Laura Forrester

Reproduction by Modern Age Repro House Ltd, Hong Kong
Printed and bound by Craft Print International Pte Ltd,
Singapore.

ISBN 1 84330 329 9

PHOTOGRAPHIC CREDITS:

John Baxter: Cover – Front, Spine, Back (Top &
Middle-Bottom); pp 2; 6–10; 12–13; 18–23; 26–29;
32–33; 42–45; 50–51; 56–57; 60–63; 66–67; 72–73;
80–81; 84–87; 90; 93

Laura Forrester: Cover – Back (Middle-Top & Bottom);
pp 5; 11; 14–17; 30–31; 34–41; 46–47; 52–55; 58–59;
64–65; 68–71; 74–79; 82–83; 88–89; 91; 95

Alan Jefferis: pp 48–49

Pat Jones: pp 24–25

BY THE SAME AUTHOR:

The Appleby Rai. Travelling people on a thousand-year
journey. Photographs by John Baxter.
Village Cricket, the genuine article. Photographs by
John Baxter.
43 Unsporting Moments. Illustrations by Paul Davies.
The Buxton Baths Murders.

The shed artists and craftsmen may be contacted via
the Publishers.